Rottweilers as Pets

The Ultimate Guide for Rottweilers

Rottweilers General Info, Purchasing, Care, Cost, Keeping, Health, Supplies, Food, Breeding and More Included!

By Lolly Brown

Foreword

Rottweilers are not just known for having a robust body structure, they are as well remarkable for being a courageous, confident, and loyal type of companion but it may not be the best choice for everyone. Before putting into conclusion whether or not this breed might be right for you and your family, you must first make yourself familiar with this dog breed. You have to gather round sufficient information, and devote your time and effort in able to know this dog breed.

This book will tackle all the necessary information you need to know about Rottweilers; from their heritage, physique, down to their special and specific needs in terms of its health, nutrition, grooming, habitat, maintenance, and well-being.

Table of Contents

Introduction

The Rottweilers are known for being a loyal, trainable, and a great companion and these characteristics make them a great guard dog. Even before time, this breed is responsible for herding the cattle of Roman soldiers and helping the butcher bring the meat to the market. See, even history is an eye witness on how responsible and reliable Rottweilers are.

Rottweilers are very trainable too. They are very clever dogs who enjoy physical and mental training. They can also be very affectionate and can get along with other animals especially if they have been socialized properly at a very young age. They are territorial and will do everything to protect their owner and family.

But before you bring a Rottweiler home make sure that you are mental, emotionally, physically, and financially ready in order to take care of your new pet properly. Always remember that the welfare of your dog is very important and it is essential to provide them a happy and healthy life. In order to make it possible, you must first become knowledgeable of the breed you are about to acquire.

In addition to the general information, biological background, and physical attributes of Rottweilers, this book will also delve deeper on how to take care of Rottweiler in terms of its nutrition, health, grooming, maintenance, and habitat. You will also be provided with information as to how to properly breed them along with the criteria for showing. Pros and cons will also be given including some links to resources that will help you to understand fully the breed you are dealing with

We hope that this book will be of great help for you as a newbie, or even for those already have an experience in taking care of dog already. Enjoy!

Chapter One: Biological Information

Rottweilers are not just known for having a robust body structure, they are as well remarkable for being a courageous, confident, and loyal type of companion but it may not be the best choice for everyone. Before putting into conclusion whether or not this breed might be right for you and your family, you must first make yourself familiar with this dog breed. You have to gather round sufficient information, and devote your time and effort in able to know this dog breed.

Found in this chapter, is an introduction to the breed which includes some basic biological facts and general information along with the history of how it came about. This information, along with the practical information about keeping in the next chapter, will assist you in deciding if this is the perfect breed for you.

Taxonomy

The Rottweilers have a scientific name of *Canis Familiaris*. They belong in Kingdom *Animalia*, Phylum *Chordata*, Class *Mammalia*, Order *Carnivora*, Family *Canidae*, Genus *Canis*, and Species *Lupus Familiaris*.

Origin and History

It is believed that Rottweilers originally came from Germany where they are known as Rottweiler Metzgerhund which means Rottweil butchers' dogs as they assist in herding livestock and pulling carts filled with butchered meat all the way to the market. They are also a part of Roman cattle dogs which had escorted the herds behind the wake of Roman armies.

In 74 AD, the 11th Legion of the Roman Empire set camp in Wurtemberg, Germany by the bank of the river Neckar. Years passed, the area became a little town filled with small villas roofed by red tiles. It became known as *das*

Rote Wil – 'rot' originating from the red roof tiles and 'wil' from the villa. From then on, the city full of red-roofed Roman villas was eventually called 'Rottweil.'

At some point in the Middle Ages, Rottweilers were exploited to hunt for wild bears and subsequently given the responsibility to control cattle. They have to watch the herd at night to preclude any cattle from straying, to lead the herd as they go long distances by day, and to protect the crusade against possible predators like dangerous bulls. Rottweilers were bred to be resilient and robust, parallel to the breed known today.

In the year 1899, the International Club for Leonbergers and Rottweiler Dogs was established in Germany. This club has set the first breed standard for the Rottweiler in 1901.

With the advancement of the area during the 19th century, railways came and cattle herding was prohibited by law. The Rottweilers were then left with no occupation. And so, the butchers had them as draughts dogs, pulling little carts filled with meat. They became known as Rottweii Butcher's Dog, as mentioned earlier, that later shortened to Rottweiler.

In 1907, a club dedicated to safeguarding the well-being of the breed started planned breeding and put up other efforts to improve the appearance and to preserve the working qualities of the breed. Another Rottweiler governing body, The Allgemeiner Deutscher Rottweiler Klub or ADRK, was established in the year 1922.

Physical Traits

Rottweilers are medium-to-large size dogs that weigh an average of 95-130 lbs. for males and 85-115 lbs. for females. It stands at the height of 24"- 27" for males and 22"-25" for females with a life span of 10 years or more varying on how you take care of its health.

They have a large and broad head and defined athletic, muscular body. Their chest is deep reaching the level of their elbows and their back is straight. They have small triangular ears that lie flat to the head and a wide black nose. They own a deep set of almond-shaped dark brown eyes. Their nails are black in color. They are covered with smooth and glossy black coat, medium in length, coarse to the touch, with a hint of tan markings on the chest, legs, cheeks, and muzzle. The outer coat is flat and dense while the inner coat covers only their neck and thighs.

They are not naturally without tails. Tails were customarily being removed to avoid future infections caused by mud and other debris coming from livestock and pastures.

Quick Facts

Origin: Germany

Breed Size: medium-to-large size breed

Body Type and Appearance: Has an athletic muscular body and a large and broad head

Group: Allgemeiner Deutscher Rottweiler Klub (ADRK), International Club for Leonbergers and Rottweiler Dogs, American Rottweiler Club

Height: 24"- 27" for males and 22"- 25" for females

Weight: an average of 95-130 lbs. for males and 85-115 lbs. for females

Coat Length: medium-length coat

Coat Texture: smooth and glossy, coarse to touch

Color: Black with a hint of tan markings on the chest, legs, cheeks, and muzzle

Temperament: ranging from serious, reserved, and self-assured to affectionate and silly

Strangers: territorial therefore aloof with strangers and can be aggressive towards them

Other Dogs: can be aggressive especially towards the dog of the same sex

Other Pets: can get along with other pets but some are predatory towards cats.

Training: clever, easy to train, very responsive

Exercise Needs: daily brisk walks, romping sessions

Health Conditions: generally healthy but are prone to common health problems including bloat, panosteitis, elbow dysplasia, cataracts, osteochondritis, Von Willebrand's diseases, diabetes, progressive retinal atropy, aortic stenosis, colitis

Lifespan: average 10- 12 years

Other name: Rottie, Rottweiler Metzgerhund

Chapter Two: Rottweilers as Pets

After familiarizing yourself with some information about Rottweilers like their historical background, their physical characteristics, and how they were once Germany's most in demand pet, it's now the perfect time for you to see if this breed would be the best choice not only for you but for your family as well.

Through the help of this chapter, you will get a set of new information on the pros and cons of having a Rottweiler as a pet, the legal requirements to be met in order keep one, how this breed deals with other pets, its personalities and behaviors, and some reasons why one would consider it as great pet.

Is A Rottweiler an Ideal Pet For You?

A dog and its owner should get along as they will spend most of their time together. Having said that, if you're planning to buy and have a Rottweiler as your pet, you must make sure that both of your personalities match well. It is vital that both your disposition and characteristics jive well with your chosen pet in order for you to find delight in each other's company.

To help you figure out your compatibility with Rottweilers, we'll give you an overview of their behavioral characteristics or temperament, the cost of owning one and also how you can acquaint them or introduce them to your other pets if any.

Temperament and Behavioral Characteristics

Rottweilers are loyal, courageous, and clever pets. Having these characteristics makes them excellent watchdogs that are always ready to protect the family where they belong. Some of them are aloof while others are very playful. Their behavior actually depends on how they were trained and raised by their owners.

They are muscular dogs who are in need of physical activities to keep them active. They tend to get bored easily and sometimes destroy and chew on things when they do not exercise enough. Regular walks and romping sessions are the usual bodily training they need. They are very clever dogs, and so, mental exercises are also vital. It is highly recommended to train Rottweilers while they're young to ensure that you'll be able to shape them properly and let them learn the right traits.

These dogs are naturally territorial. They have an inherent desire to safeguard their family and property. The sex of the dogs often affects their behavior. The males are very watchful, frequently assessing threats while the females are to some degree more affectionate and easygoing.

If you want to work well with this dog breed, you have to ensure that you'll be a confident owner who's got the ability to take charge of this strong-minded pet. You have to give them respect and must be able to attend to their basic needs, as well as their need for affection. You must ensure that your pet knows that you are still the one in charge and, at the same time, they should feel that they are loved and properly sheltered.

Behavioral Characteristics with other Pets

This type of dogs can be friendly with other household pets such as cats, other dog breeds, or the likes if they are properly socialized, introduced, and exposed to other pets found in your home from a young age. It basically depends on the upbringing of the Rottweiler itself.

Initially, they can be potentially aggressive with other animals especially to other dogs of the same sex as they are inherently protective and see others as a threat. But, if given enough time to socialize with other animals, they'll be able to know what lines they can, and cannot cross. With the help of proper training, they will be able to distinguish a threatening situation from a non-threatening one.

Pros and Cons of Rottweilers

Pros

- They are courageous, smart, loyal, obedient, and devoted to their family.
- They are powerful, very intelligent and trainable.
- They have a medium-length coat that is considered low maintenance and they don't shed excessively.
- Gets along with other pets, if provided with enough socialization and exposure to others.
- A good companion; affectionate and safeguards its owner and the family it belongs
- Great for households who have children
- A good running or hiking buddy

Cons

- Not your typical house pet. Demands outdoor activities.
- They are needed to be monitored as they overeat if given the chance
- Destruct things when bored or when they haven't exercised enough.
- They can be aggressive toward other animals
- Keeping them can be a bit pricey (supplies and medical expenses)

- Prone to serious health problems and conditions

Dog Licensing

If you love travelling and you want to bring your dog with you, you must pay attention to this segment. There are certain restrictions and regulations that you have to be mindful of when you are planning to bring your pet to your trip. Licensing requirements for pets differ in various countries, regions, and states so you must check into it to avoid problems.

Some countries, however, do not require licensing for dogs but despite the fact that most states do not have a mandatory requirement for people to license their dogs, it is still the best idea to do so as it will not only benefit your pet but it will also do good for you in terms of protection.

Common Licensing Questions (U.S. Breeders)

- Does the United States require dog licensing?
United States are one of those countries that has no federal requirements for licensing dogs but still licensing is needed as it is regulated at the state level. Licensing requirements differ from one state to another, but most

states do mandatorily require dog owners to register and license their dogs.

- What are the requirements needed in the United States for dog licensing?

  Documentary requirements must be presented before you can avail a pet license such as current rabies vaccination certificate. In some states, they require additional documents before the release of the permanent license. For the meantime, the license will be deemed temporary until all requirements are received and once you've been given the license you will then have the need to renew it each year as well as your dog's rabies vaccination.

- How much will it cost?

  Usually, dog licenses only cost about $25 per annum.

- Why should I prefer to license my dog?

  Although the state or region you belong does not require mandatory licensing of dogs, you must still consider acquiring one. When you get a license for your dog will be given a dog number that is linked to your contact information so that if your dog gets lost, for whatever reason it will be easier to find it. If someone has seen your dog, its license can be used to find and contact you so that they'll be able to return your pet to you. This will only be made possible if your dog is wearing a collar with an ID tag. So make sure you take this measure.

Common Licensing Questions (U.K. Breeders)

- Does the United Kingdom require dog licensing?
  In the United Kingdom, it required for the dog owners to register and license their pet dog. Owning an unlicensed dog in the UK is considered an offense unless the puppy is six months old or younger, it's a police dog, if it's kept for sale in a licensed pet store, it's under block license or if it's assistance dog accompanying a person with a disability. Other than that, domestic pet dogs are required by law to be licensed individually.

- How much would it cost?
  A dog license costs £12.50 and lasts for 12 months and is subjected for renewal. You can find an application form for a dog license and dog license renewal over your local council's website or you can personally apply to your council offices.

- Is there a need for me to license each of them if I have more than one dog?

  If by chance you're owning three or more dogs, you may apply for the so called "block license" costing £32. This type of license is available as long as there are at least three unsterilized bitches breeding less than three litters over a year or in which at least three dogs are registered guard dog kennels of the following bodies:

  - Irish Coursing Club
  - Kennel Club
  - International Sheep Dog Society
  - Masters of Harriers and Beagles Association
  - Northern Ireland Masters of Hounds Association
  - Masters of Foxhounds Association

General Licensing Guidelines

If you are going to bring your dog to another country besides US and UK, it is advisable to make a research on the requirements and country laws, with regards to bringing dogs, of the place you're wishing to visit and also of the airlines you're traveling with. Usually, proper documents such as the state license of your dog, vaccination certificates, and other papers reflecting the health condition of your dog will be needed.

Costs of Owning a Dog

In this section, you will be given an overview of the expenses associated with purchasing and keeping dogs as you must be willing to cover these costs. The expenses you'll initially encounter includes the cost of the dog itself as well as its bed, accessories, toys, initial vaccinations, micro-chipping or licensing, spay/neuter surgery plus grooming supplies.

Are You Financially Prepared?

Having pets, in general, can be expensive whether it's a low maintenance or a high maintenance one. Either of the two, you need to provide them enough supplies essential for them to keep up with a healthy lifestyle and you must make available a dog-friendly environment.

Though it looks simple, these little things will definitely become an additional line item to your daily budget. The entire cost of these dog-related expenses will vary depending on where you buy the supplies, the brand it belongs, the amount of nutrients present, the time being, etc.

If you are really dedicated to owning a Rottweiler, you must be willing to cover these costs.

The expenses you'll initially encounter includes the cost of the dog itself as well as its bed, accessories, toys, initial vaccinations, micro- chipping or licensing, spay/neuter surgery plus grooming supplies.

Average Price of Rottweilers

The average price for a Rottweiler varies depending on its kind and where you acquire it. A show quality/ breedable puppy's cost ranges approximately $2,500- $4,000 depending on the bloodline, age, and titles owned while a pet quality/non-breedable puppy costs approximately $2,000. Additional costs are demanded if shipping is required. These are the expenses you might come across if you are going to purchase from a reputable breeder. In the case of shelter dogs, you can avail them for as low as $100 for a puppy and $400 or more for an adult.

Take note that the cost of Rottweiler varies depending on the age, quality of the breed, the vaccinations it received, the cage it comes with as well as the accessories. In some stores, they require deposit or reservation fee especially when the dog is not ready to be brought home yet.

Other Dog Essentials

Apart from its purchase price, there's also a need to buy supplementary things like dishes, toy, beds, grooming necessities, supplements and food supplies. You need to reserve enough budgets to cover for vaccinations especially for puppies, along with other expenses like license renewal, microchipping, vet consultations, spay/neuter procedures and other needed accessories.

- **Bed:** Rottweilers are medium-to-large– size dogs which are why a normal sized dog bed or even a larger one can suit your pet. Normally, the average cost for a normal size dog bed is actually around $50 - $200.

- **Food and water bowl:** It is recommended that the material composing the food/water bowl is stainless steel for the reason that it is easier to clean, cannot be destroyed chewed or eaten by your pet and it won't acquire bacteria. A quality set of stainless steel bowls can be acquired at about $30.

- **Toys:** Rottweilers are an inherently active type of dogs and toys are a vital part of any dog's physical and mental exercise. Initially, it's advisable for you to purchase toys of different kinds until you learn what toy your pet prefers. You can spend $25 up to $150 per year. It is also recommended to acquire toys designated for "tough chewers" as Rottweilers have the capability to chew on toys destructively.

- **Food and Healthy Treats:** It is essential to feed your dog with nothing but of high-quality dog food and healthy dog treats. Food expenses differ depending on the size, energy level, and activities of your dog. The quality and the brand of food also give the variation towards this expense. For a Rottweiler, the typical cost for food is approximate $40-$60 per month. Make sure that your pet gets only high-quality food. It may look expensive but the nutrients it can give to your dog can actually make them stronger and less prone to any illness just like helping you save bucks from any medication.

- **Other accessories/tools:** Since this dog breed requires physical activities or else they'll get bored, you have to take them for a walk daily. Therefore, you need at least one leash and one collar with ID tags. The cost for leashes and collars depend on the quality and size. It's very important to invest on high-quality collars and leashes since it will help you save money in the long run. Owners spend $20-$50 on these accessories per year. Grooming tools are also a must-have. It might only cost you as low as $30-$250 per year since this breed has smooth coated and short-haired.

Medical Expenses

Medical expenses such as initial vaccinations for puppies, microchipping, spay/neuter surgery, and the occasional consultations to the vet should also be well-thought-out as part of your budget for your pet

Microchipping for Your Pet

Safety of a pet is every owner's concern. Luckily, there are ways to ensure the well-being of your dog especially against the probability of getting lost and one of it is microchipping.

Microchipping is a process of implanting a microchip under your dog's skin bearing a number that is associated with your contact information. If ever your dog will be lost, the founder shall bring your pet on the nearest shelter and within just a scan, they'll be able to track you down and help you be reunited with your pet.

This procedure takes just a few minutes to perform and it only costs about $30-$50 on average, but the price may differ depending on where the procedure is done. In some states there can be other documents required that you may need to submit to your local government.

Vaccination for Pups

This cost is only applicable if you purchased a puppy in its early stage of life. A number of different vaccinations are needed by your pet. If you acquired your puppy from a highly regarded breeder, it might already have a few shots but you'll still need to keep a substantial amount for more necessary vaccination over the next few months along with booster shots needed every year.

Rottweilers can still be prone to certain viral and bacterial infections. At any time, emergencies may arise so just to be sure that your pet is safe; you may need to provide these vaccinations to keep their health in good condition.

Also if your dog received appropriate boosters they need, at their early life, it can help lengthen their life expectancy. You should definitely consider this in your budget which may cost you at approximately $50 or more.

Spay/Neuter Surgery

If you are not planning to breed your Rottweiler, you may want to consider having them neutered if it's a male or spayed if it's a female. This procedure involves the process of ssurgically removing the testicles of a male dog and removing the ovaries and uterus of the female. This may prevent any unwanted pregnancies and also other certain types of cancer. Usually this is performed before your dog turn 6 months of age to give the maximum protection against any reproductive order diseases.

Usually spay/ neuter surgery costs $50 to $100 and spays surgery costs about $100 to $200. But this may vary on the gender of your dog and where the procedure will be done. A traditional veterinary surgeon could be expensive but if you want a cheaper one you can bring your pet to a veterinary clinic.

Veterinary Consultations

Veterinary Care plays a huge part in keeping your dog healthy. It is advisable to plan a visit to the vet at least twice a year. It cost for about $200-$500 yearly.

Chapter Three: Purchasing and Selecting a Healthy Breed

Selecting a healthy Rottweiler breed as well as a trustworthy and highly regarded breeder is a very tricky part. You must be paying attention on all the details no matter how big or small it is to ensure that you are on the right track. Factors like who takes care of them and the manner they are taken care of, especially if they're still puppies are some of the things you have to consider in buying one. With the help of this chapter, you will learn how to depict to whom and where to purchase a Rottweiler breed.

Best Places to Acquire a Rottweiler Breed

There are lots of places where you can purchase a Rottweiler. In this section, you will learn both of its advantages and disadvantages. Measure up one from the other and see for yourself that best suits you.

Pet Stores

Advantages of Buying a Rottweiler in a Pet Store

- It's the easiest and most convenient place to look for a loving pet.
- Pet stores can provide "purebred" puppies at a much lower price.
- Pet store owners guarantee the health of the puppies they sell and usually these puppies own proper documentation.

Disadvantages of Buying a Rottweiler in a Pet Store

- The pets, specifically puppies, are most often supplied by puppy mills wherein puppies are kept in such despicable conditions making them more prone to infection and catching an illness.

- Dogs from pet stores usually have behavioral problems since at a very young age they are separated from their parent and are house broken.
- They were raised in a small cage making them hyperactive with a chance of barking excessively.
- Continuing to buy on local pet shops is like supporting a bad industry since according to many breeders, pet stores are not taking care of such pets. As you've emptied one cage, another demand is created and the owners will just re-stock these pet stores.

Reputable Breeders

Advantages of Buying A Rottweiler from Private Breeders

- You'll be able to determine whether or not they are reputable breeders since they are the ones taking care of the puppies first hand.
- You can negotiate with them regarding the price that best fits your budget.
- You can also ask for some pointers on how to take care and get along with the breed since they are well knowledgeable about the temperament of these puppies.

Disadvantages of Buying a Rottweiler from Private Breeders

- Acquiring dogs from private breeder is that you have to personally visit the location where these animals are being bred just to check whether they are of good repute or not.
- If ever you have decided to purchase them already, you have to pick them up for yourself which is a major drawback especially if you live in an area far from it.

Online Pet Stores

Advantages of Buying a Rottweiler through Online Pet Stores

- There are lots of advertisements posted online from private advertisers in different pet websites which is a convenient way to find a pet.
- You'll be able to find a dog beforehand without the need to travel to the location.

Disadvantages of Buying a Rottweiler through Online Pet Stores

- You can't be really sure if the dog shown in the advertisement is in good health condition just by checking photos or videos found on the website.

- To be sure if these dogs are well bred, you may need to visit personally the breeder which is not advisable if your area is far from its location and it will be a waste of time if you discovered that it's not a reputable breeder after driving a long way.

Dog Conventions

Advantages of Buying a Rottweiler on Dog Conventions

- This is a fantastic place to purchase for the reason that the people who attend in these kinds of events are dog enthusiasts and highly regarded breeders.
- In here, you can be sure of the breed's quality along with vaccination papers and/or proper licensing requirements.
- You'll get to come across other dog breeders and pet owners.

Disadvantages of Buying a Rottweiler on Dog Conventions

- Dog Conventions aren't a daily thing. You have to wait for months for the next event and this can be a problem if you want to buy a dog immediately.
- There can be a huge traffic of potential dog owners you might come across.

Characteristics of a Reputable Breeder

After knowing where to buy your dog, it's time to determine who to buy it from. Opting for a breeder is the first step before you buy any pet because if the breeder is reputable, caring, and a responsible one, you can be sure that the dog or breeds are well – taken care of. Here are the following parameters you must consider for you to be able to choose a dog breeder of good standing:

- Ask for referrals. Inquire in veterinary offices, pet stores, and groomers for Rottweiler breeders.
- Check out the website for each breeder included on your list and look for the breeder's history, experience, registration in national or local breed club, and other essential information.
- If the website you visited lacks information, don't waste your time and move on to the next breeder on your list.
- Try to contact the breeder and ask questions about their experience and knowledge with regards to breeding a Rottweiler.
- Ask for specific information about the breeding stock including the breeding program they use, registration numbers, and health information

- When the breeder asks questions about yourself, it's a sign that he is an accountable breeder making sure that his dogs go to good hands.
- Request for a tour of the facilities from several breeders to make sure that they are accommodating healthy-looking puppies.
- If the facilities don't look well, tick off the breeder from your list.
- See to it that the breeder offers health guarantees and inquire about any vaccinations the puppies/dogs may already have.
- Narrow down your list and choose the best breeder available
- Put down a deposit if it is needed to reserve a puppy if they aren't ready to be picked up.

What Indicates a Healthy Breed?

The succeeding portion is the most essential and fun part! After being aware and gaining knowledge where to buy a dog, and who to buy from, it's the moment in time to choose your very own Rottweiler. Given that you have already decided that a Rottweiler is the ideal pet for you, it's now time to check whether your dog you're about to spend your time with is not only physically healthy but it also exceptional with comes to behavior and personality

Here is a checklist with the things you have to consider for you to be able to select a healthy Rottweiler breed:

Checklist about the Dog's Physical Appearance

- ✓ Check the dog's coat color and texture
- ✓ Examine the dog's body for any signs of illness and potential injuries.
- ✓ Check its body parts and look for any sign of abnormality
- ✓ Check the dog's back legs and see if there's any sign of dysplasia
- ✓ The dog's ears and nasal passage should be clean, and clear with no discharge or inflammation.
- ✓ The dog's eyes should have clear, almond shaped bright eyes with no signs discharge.
- ✓ Check for the teeth and gums and make sure they are also in a good condition.
- ✓ Ensure that the dog is active and free from any signs of infection.

Check list about the Dog's Temperament

- ✓ The puppy should not be overly shy and it should be friendly and lets you handle them.
- ✓ To determine the behavior of the puppy, observe them from the litter box of your selection and look at how it interacts with other dogs.

- ✓ You can call them over, pet and play with them to check how they socialize with humans.
- ✓ Try holding them or picking them up to see if they are how they react with human contact. If they are too scared or if they shy away it indicates that they aren't properly socialized.
- ✓ If you haven't seen any problems with all of the puppies, it suggests that the breeder is responsible and reliable and all you have to do is to choose the puppy that captured your heart.

List of Breeders and Rescue Websites

Finding a reputable breeder is very critical as there are many claiming and pretending that they are, hence, you can never be sure of it unless you do your own extensive research to verify their claims. But before purchasing Rottweiler puppy, you may want to take into consideration if it will be better for you to just adopt a Rottweiler than to but one. Actually, there's a large population of adult Rottweilers who's been maltreated and abandoned by their previous owners, looking for a new home and family.

Reasons Why You Should Consider Adopting Dogs

- Adopting a dog is also like saving their lives and giving them a new hope.
- It can be less expensive than buying from a breeder
- The adopting agencies let you bring home your dog along with its cage and other accessories which can save you bucks.
- Some of the adult dogs up for adoption have been already litter trained socialized, and vaccinated.

To help you narrow down your choices, here is a list of breeders and adoption rescue websites around the United States and the United Kingdom you may opt to look into:

United States Breeders and Rescue Websites

Southern States Rescued Rottweilers
< www.southernstatesrescuedrottweilers.org/>

American Rottweiler Club
< www.amrottclub.org/>

Guardian Rottweilers
< guardianrottweilers.com/>

Rottie Aid Rottweiler Rescue
< www.rottieaid.org/>

Rotts 'n Pups Rescue Inc.
< www.rottsnpupsrescue.org/>

German Rottweiler Breeders
< www.lonecreekrottweilers.com/>

Rottweiler Breeders Tennessee

D.E.L.T.A Rescue
< www.deltarescue.org>

Vail Mountain Rescue Group
< www.vailmountainrescue.org/>

Von Evman Rottweilers
< https://vonevmans.com/>

Spirit Acres Farm
< www.spiritacres.org/>

Rotten Rottie Rescue
< www.rottenrottie.com/>

Southern Alberta Rottweiler Rescue
< www.albertarottweilers.com/>

United Kingdom Breeders and Rescue Websites

Pet Adoption UK
< www.petadoptionuk.co.uk/>

Rottweiler Rescue Trust

< www.rottweilerrescuetrust.co.uk/>

Rottweiler Welfare

< https://rottweilerwelfare.co.uk/>

The Kennel Club

< www.thekennelclub.org.uk/>

Varenka Rottweilers

< www.varenka.co.uk/>

Rottweiler Rescue and Rehoming

< www.fiferottweilerrescue.co.uk/>

Pendley Rottweilers

< www.pendleyrottweilers.co.uk/>

Gouldryck Rottweilers

< www.gouldryckrottweilers.co.uk/>

Chapter Four: Habitat Requirements for Rottweilers

The environment your Rottweiler lives in is a great factor you must consider as it can affect the mood and behavior of your pet. It is vital for you to provide them with the best place to dwell in order to keep your dog happy and satisfied with the new environment it belongs. In this chapter, you learn the basics of how to keep your place a dog friendly one. You will also be made aware of the things your pet needs including its shelter and other essential accessories. Some tips on how to properly dog- proof your house and some guidelines on how you can preserve an appropriate living condition for them will be provided.

Habitat Requirements

Rottweilers need a secure large area intended for both exercise and play. Space is a vital factor to consider due to the size of this breed. The place where the dog will stay during idle time is also something you should take into account.

Dog Bed vs. Shelter/Cages

Dogs like Rottweilers do not only need a big dog bed but also a durable and sturdy one. The bigger the bed you buy for your pet, the more economical it will be especially if you acquire a puppy since it will save you bucks from buying a bigger bed when it grows. You must be meticulous in choosing a dog bed. Make sure that the cushions are comfortable and are made from high-quality materials. You can buy dog beds from well-known and excellent brands to be certain that it will last for a long time. You can also provide them sheets and even small pillows to make it cozier.

Pets differ from one another. There are dogs that favor sleeping on the floor or on a mat rather than on a cozy dog bed. If that's the case, don't push them too hard to sleep on the bed you purchased. Remember that they are still in the period of adjustment. As time goes by they'll learn and they'll take sleeping on dog beds as their preference.

Quick tip:

If you want to encourage your dog to sleep in the bed, you could drop its favorite toy on it to make it more appealing. If your dog lies down on its bed, you can give him treats, another reward, or even a compliment along with a tap on its head.

If you're planning to let your dog stay in a cage it's also advisable for you to buy a bigger cage as for its economic benefits. Purchasing a cage for your pet is at your own discretion. There will be times that your dog will not want to go and stay inside its cage. It is recommended that you let your Rottweiler roam around and socialize with other pets or human beings to avoid them from developing an aggressive behavior.

Buying a cage or shelter for your dog can be a little hassle for you especially if you have lots of other responsibilities hanging around since owning such requires daily cleaning as you don't want it to accumulate any bacteria, dirt, or other creatures like ants. Unlike if you buy a dog bed, you can easily clean it by washing or you can even bring it to the laundry. On the other hand, if you have plenty of pets you can prefer having cages/shelters to avoid territorial clash among them.

Play Pen, Toys, and Other Accessories

Playing time plays a vital role in the mental and physical development of Rottweilers and so you must make sure that your dog gets adequate time and certain accessories it needs to further intensify the quality of its playing time. It can also be a good chance to spend time and bond with your pet. It will benefit both you and your pet.

Providing a play pen for your dog is something you should consider in doing. Dogs, in general, are energetic in nature. They are such active and playful creatures. But you have to keep in mind that your pet might get hurt with all the energy it contains, not only that, there is also a possibility that they might break something or even get lost. And so, to avoid these possible hazards that might come across your dog's playtime, a decent playpen structured for giving a safe environment offers just that.

Dog playpens come in a variety of sizes. The bigger the playpen the more your dog will get to exercise and play around as if he's free and not inside a confined area. It can be utilized both indoors and outdoors. If you're going to buy a playpen, make sure that you consider the size of it as dogs don't want to be always cooped up in a cage or room without space to play. Take note that it must be spacious and enjoyable for your pet.

Generally, dogs need something to play with to keep them from boredom. Rottweilers are fond of toys that keep them physically and mentally stimulated since this breed is naturally playful and get easily bored when doing nothing. In that case, you should consider furnishing them with such. As to buying toys for your Rottweiler, make sure that these are all ultra-durable toys as they can potentially destruct and chew on toys easily.

Housing Temperature

The temperature is an environmental factor you have to consider for your dogs. Different dog breeds vary in the temperature ranges they are most comfortable with. In the case of Rottweilers, they prefer cold more than hot weather. They should not be exposed where the temperature is more than 35 C. The temperature that fits with its tolerance is ranging from 0 C to 25 C. Also, avoid putting your dog under direct sunlight as it may cause serious harm to them.

Keeping Your Dog Safe Around the House

If your pet hasn't arrived yet and if you're way too excited for its arrival, you can try to make your home dog-friendly or dog-proof for the meantime. By this process, you will be able to protect your pet from various household hazards and be able to steer them away from any potential unwanted accidents or situations. You should not only provide a happy environment for your dog but you must also make sure that you'll be able to achieve a safe place for them to live. Below are some courses of action on how to dog – proof your home as well as how to keep them happy.

- Keep away food that can highly intoxicate your dog like macadamia nuts, chocolate, grapes, raisins, etc. It is best if you store them where your pet could not reach it.
- Store away hazardous chemicals like cleaners, fabric softeners, bleach, etc. that can be dangerous if swallowed.
- Keep medications on high shelves
- Put into a secure area any objects that might suffocate your pet like plastic bags and plastic bags.
- Keep the towels and stray socks away from your pet's reach as they may get tempted to chew on it that can lead them in developing gastrointestinal problems.

- Put up a screen on your fireplace as your dog can get harmed by flying ashes or even on the flames itself.
- Dogs get tempted to chew on things so it's best to tuck electrical cords away to prevent electrocution.
- Always supervise and keep an eye on your dog as it may reach the part of your house that can be dangerous for them like the kitchen and bathroom.
- Provide fences to make sure that your dog won't slip out.
- Keep trash cans securely closed so that your dog won't be able to get into the garbage.
- Install childproof latches on cabinets as your pets might get curious and accidentally open them.
- Put away breakable items that your pet might knock over.
- Keep your sharp tools away from your pet's reach.
- Make sure that the plants you're having in your garden are not poisonous and safe for dogs.
- Put the dog toys out and keep anything precious and destructible away.
- Spend quality time with your dog. Teach him new tricks and train his obedience.
- Play with your dog and build a good relationship with your pet.

Chapter Five: Nutrition and Feeding

Every pet owner should be very hands on when it comes to the proper nutrition of his pet. Rottweilers are not complicated to feed but there are factors like age, weight, and level of activity that should never be compromised. It is very important for your dog to meet its nutritional diet needs in order to live a life away from any serious illness and with a longer life expectancy. Therefore, it is a must to provide your dog a balanced nutrition.

In this portion, you'll be made knowledgeable of your pet's nutritional needs along with some feeding guidelines, foods that are best and can be harmful to your dog, and also a review of various brands of dog foods for Rottweilers.

Nutritional Needs of Rottweilers

It is every pet owner's responsibility to ensure that his dog is living a happy and healthy life and the best way to achieve this is through a healthy diet. Let's take a peek on what we can feed our Rottweilers to provide them the nutrition they need.

Rottweilers are carnivores in nature. This means that they primarily eat meat. To provide the best nutrition for your dog, you should let them consume meat mainly in their diet, by this way, you also to be able to control their weight. This is a problem when you look at the ingredients found on a bag of dog foods. In there, you'll see that the ingredient composing the dog food is primarily grains. One reason is that meat is more expensive than grains. So you better keep an eye on this.

Your Rottweiler needs a meal that has lots of protein. A puppy should be served with a meal that contains 24%-28% protein. On the other hand, an adult Rottweiler needs food that contains 22%- 26% protein. A high protein diet is what your pet needs to keep them from becoming overweight for the reason that proteins are not stored as fat but rather excreted through kidneys. It is essential for puppies to consume more protein in their diet as it plays a vital role in the development of their muscles and strength. The fat present in your dog's meal should only be in a small amount or else your dog will become overweight. The amount of fat healthy for a puppy should only be 14% - 18% and 12% to 16% for an adult.

The main ingredient in the dog food you have to purchase should be meat or meal meat. If it contains chicken, herring meal, chicken meal, turkey meal, and the likes, it will best suit your dog. Take note that if you want to provide your pet with a proper diet, never feed them with food that comprised soy, corn, or wheat. Also, do not buy dog foods containing sugar, artificial color, and chemical preservatives as these ingredients can be potentially harmful to them.

Types of Standard Commercial Dog Foods

There are three major types of commercial dog foods namely canned foods, semi-moist foods, and dry foods. Let's look further at the differences between these foods and find out what best fits your pet to consume.

Canned Foods

This type of dog food consist 75% water together with assorted fish, cereal products, and fish. This type is easier to prepare and your dog will definitely enjoy this meal. The downside of this food is that it usually contains low-energy nutrients that you have to give your pet a big serving meal or even double it in order to furnish the nutrients as well as the energy he needs

Semi-moist foods

This food only contains 15%- 30% of water and has a high concentration. Semi-moist dog foods provide more amount of energy even in a less amount of volume, unlike canned foods. Plus, it's easier to digest. This type of food need not be refrigerated, more convenient, and comes in a wide variety you can choose from.

The negative aspect of this kind of dog food is that it is expensive and contains corn syrup and sugar that might be harmful to your dog especially those who have diabetes. It also has artificial flavors and colorings.

Dry Foods

This type of food provides a high energy value and contains only 10% water. Of all the types of commercial dog foods, this one is the least expensive. Many dog owners consider buying this in bulk orders and consider this as an economical way to feed their dogs. However, these types of dog food are loaded with mostly cereals and contain a very limited amount of protein. You can consider mixing canned foods with dry foods to make the meal a balanced one. You can also look for a dry food that has meat as its main ingredient.

Recommended Brands of Rottweilers Dog Foods

If you want to provide the best nutrients for you Rottweiler, you must not only focus on the type of food but also the brand that produces it. You must be meticulous on what brand to trust with regards of the meal of your loving pet. Below is a list of 5 most notable brands recommended and you can choose from in providing the nutritional diet needs of your dog.

#1: Blue Buffalo Wilderness Salmon Recipe

This brand provides a grain-free dry dog food. It contains peas, potatoes, and sweet potatoes that offer complex carbohydrates healthy for your dog. It also has carrots, cranberries, and blueberries that provide antioxidants. The protein component of this dog food is provided by the deboned salmon, dish meal, and chicken meal present in this product. There are no grains, wheat, soy, corn, artificial flavors, colors, and preservatives mixed in this food that can be potentially harmful to your pet.

The benefits that your dog can get from this product are healthy muscle growth, strong bones and teeth, healthy skin and shiny coat, plus it supports a healthy immune system. You can avail a 24lb package from this brand of dog food for as low as $50.

#2: I and Love and You Nude Food Red Meat

This one is a high-protein and grain-free kibble that caters real pork as the main ingredient. It provides an exclusive blend of prebiotics, probiotics, and digestive enzymes perfect for improving and easing digestion. It contains deboned meat as well as real fruits and vegetables. It is fortified with omega-3 and 6 fatty acids that make its coat shine. It is loaded with turmeric, coconut oil, and flaxseeds that provide the necessary nutrients for your dog. It is made with premium ingredients and contains no harmful ingredients like wheat, soy, and corn. You can avail this product for as low as $45 per 23-lb bag.

#3: Innova Nature's Table Grain Free Ranch-Raised Beef & Red Lentils

This product is a meat-based and grain-free dog meal. This brand is actually highly praised by some dog owners. The high-protein ingredients that comprise this product are beef and lamb meal. These meat concentrations can really provide the protein your dog needs. It also contains red and green lentils. These are a great source of carbohydrates and fortified with natural fiber. It also has sunflower oil that is rich in omega-6 fatty acids and flaxseed notable for being a good source of omega-3 fatty acids. You can avail this product at the price of $45.

#4: Blackwood Chicken Meal & Rice Recipe

This product contains the nutrition your dog needs. Packed with premium all-natural chicken protein and contains no corn, soy, wheat, artificial color, and flavors. This product underwent the process of slow-cooking. This is a flavorful and easy to digest as it is fortified with probiotics that help ease digestion. You can purchase a 30-lb bag for as low as $50.

#5: Eukanuba Rottweiler Dog Food

This premium dog food contains calcium to strengthen the bones, proprietary levels of L-carnitine to aid for fat burning. It contains beta-carotene and vitamin E to intensify the immune system of your pet. It caters 3D Dentadefense System to help reduce tartar accumulating on the teeth of your dog in 28 days. This is formulated meticulously to meet the nutritional standards made by the AAFCO Dog Food Nutrient Profiles. You can purchase a 30-lb bag of this product for as low as $50.

Tips in Feeding Your Rottweilers

Check the nutritional content and value of the food you are about to give to your dog. Make sure that it contains enough protein, carbohydrates, and fiber.

- Purchase products with a stamp of the Association of American Feed Control Officials (AAFCO). By this way, you can ensure that the dog food you'll buy is healthy and approved by veterinarians.
- Be knowledgeable of how much food your dog needs. Make sure that you won't overfeed nor underfeed your dog.
- Put your dog's food in a bowl where he will learn to slow down like the ones with posts.
- Make sure that the food type you give to your dog has the necessary dietary needs based on their age, weight, and level of activity.
- Follow meal times as schedules. Try to feed your dog at the same time each day.
- Limit giving out treats for your dog in order to prevent obesity.
- Feed your dog in a good place reserved just for him. It is best to pick an empty corner for him to enjoy his meal without anyone or anything that will distract him

- Never forget to supply your dog with adequate water at all times. Ensure that he has access to water whenever it is necessary for him to drink. Refill his water bowl every now and then.
- Ask for your veterinarian's advice on the feeding techniques you can utilize for your pet.

Feeding Amount and Frequency

The amount and how often you need to feed your dog actually depends on its size, age, and activity level. But here are some general guidelines as to the amount and frequency of feeding your dog.

- Be sure that you feed your dog during scheduled times for them to know when to expect meals. If for example you have scheduled 3 meals per day for your 4-6-month puppy and it constantly refuses one meal, you can adjust making it 2 meals per day. Dogs over 6 months can eat 2 times a day but if there's an indication that it only needs one meal, switch into one meal per day.

- The more active your dog is the more it requires energy from food. It is recommended that your dog eats the amount of food 2-3% of its desired body weight per day. For example, if your dog weighs

100lb, you can feed them 2-3 pounds of food every day. If your dog is highly active, it needs something closer to 3% while if it has a slower metabolism 2% will do.

- Do not force your pet to eat just because you want it to grow bigger and faster.

- Ask for your veterinarian's advice as to how frequent and as to how much you should feed your dog. It still best to seek a professional's advice.

Chapter Six: Grooming and Training Your Rottweilers

After discussing proper diet and nutrition for your Rottweiler, let's now move on to another topic necessary for the well-being of your pet. We'll give you some specific guidelines as to how you can properly train and groom your dog.

Rottweilers are very trainable but they can also be stubborn at times but overall, they are easy to teach different tricks and commands especially if you'll start to train them at a very young age. In terms of grooming, you won't have any problem with them since they are average shedders for the reason that they have a short coat.

In this chapter, you'll be given some tips on how to train and keep up with their occasional naughtiness, and on how to keep them well-groomed and pleasant looking at all times.

Guidelines in Training Your Rottweilers

Training your dog is something that would benefit both you and your pet. Through it, you'll be able to build a positive and healthier relationship with your dog based on respect and mutual trust. You'll be able to teach him life skills on how to live in a home environment successfully. It helps increase your dog's sociability that will help him gain confidence, learn good manners, and prevent aggression. It is an effective way to further intensify the loyalty of your pet and its companionship.

Being able to train achieve obedience from your dog will sure feel rewarding. You don't have to spend money in training your dog, all you have to need is time and patience for your pet. Here are some general guidelines on how to train your dog:

- Let your dog recognize his own name. In this way, it will be easier to call his attention. Say his name more often whenever you are petting, training and playing with him. If you called his name and he responded quickly, it means he already learned his name.

- Schedule and spend enough time when training your dog. Set aside at least 15-20 minutes every day.

- Be sure that you are calm and ready to train your dog. It will take lots of patience in order to effectively train your dog.

- Prepare the proper equipment you need like the leash and collar.

- Whenever your dog did something great, give him a reward and praise him immediately so that he'll be able to associate the reward with the command you have given.

- You have to be consistent. Make sure that you have a clear connection with your dog and that he'll know if hit or miss your commands.

- When you're teaching your dog an important or difficult command, you may consider giving him a high-value treat.

- Do not get frustrated and reinforce each command with anger. Never raise your voice just because you want to get his attention.

- Do not feed your dog with a large meal before training, the more your dog wants the treat the more he'll be focused.

- Make sure to end each training period on a positive note. He may not be able to master all your command he'll definitely remember your love and care.

Guidelines in Grooming Your Rottweilers

Generally, Rottweiler is a "low maintenance" one when it comes to its grooming needs. Grooming is not just about keeping it clean but it is also about maintaining a healthy and shiny coat of your dog. Enjoy the time you're grooming your pet by stroking him and talking to him. Here are some general guidelines on how to bathe/groom your dog:

- Unless your Rottweiler plays in the mud or has rolled over into something that smells bad, then it does not need to be bathed frequently. You can give your dog a bath once or twice a week.

- Make sure to use a gentle and moisturizing shampoo in bathing your dog. Their skin is very sensitive and is prone to becoming dry. It is advisable that you buy a shampoo made with natural ingredients.
- It is recommended that you use a walk-in shower rather than bathing your dog in the tub.
- If you don't have any walk-in shower make sure that if you're using a tub, put a non-slip mat on it to prevent injuries.
- Make sure that the shampoo is away from his eyes and put out excess water on his ears.
- Rinse and dry the coat of your dog thoroughly using a soft cloth before letting him leave the bathroom.
- You should brush your dog's teeth more often. It is advisable that you brush it every day to prevent any dental problems.
- Make sure that you will provide a diligent dental care routine for your dog. Buy a specially designed toothbrush for your dog. Never use your regular toothpaste but rather use pet-safe toothpaste.
- Introduce the flavor of the toothpaste by putting some on your fingertip and let your dog lick it. If the dog refuses to lick it more after a few days, try to find another flavor he'll like.

- Make sure that your dog is in a spot where he is comfortable. Hold gently the lip of your dog to expose your dog's gums and teeth.
- Brush your pet's teeth using a gentle motion. Make sure that you are able to clean the canines and back molars to prevent tartar from accumulating

Trimming Your Pet's Nails and Ear Waxing

Your dog's nails grow just like any other nails. Many dogs are not fond of getting their nails cut and so trimming or clipping may never be their favorite activity but it is advisable that you let your dog get used to this routine. In cutting their nails, hold the foot gently and trim a small portion on the end of each nail. Be sure not to cut the quick or the pink part of their toenails as it supplies the blood to the nail and cutting it can cause bleeding. You can ask your veterinarian to show you how to trim them properly to the right length.

When it comes to cleaning your dog's ear, in general, the ear canals of dogs are very long and are prone to various infections. For this reason, cleaning your dog's ears is very necessary. There are many types of ear cleaners you can choose from but you should only use a dog ear cleaner of high quality. First, check if your dog's ears are inflamed, red, and itchy. If so, bring him to the vet since these are indications of infection. If not, you can proceed with this ear cleaning routine. Hand your pet a treat for sitting calmly and let him see the ear cleaner. Hold the flap of the ear gently and upright. Then put the ear cleaner inside the ear canal and gently clean the area. Afterward, use some cotton wool to wipe out the ear of your dog. Do the same steps for the other ear.

Common Dog Behaviors and How to Control Them

Dogs have the potential to learn bad habits. Instead of you getting angry and punishing them, you should try to handle it calmly. Below are some of the most common dog behaviors and the ways on how you will be able to manage them.

Digging

It is a natural canine instinct for your dog to dig and it's something that can't be shut down. So instead of getting angry, join him. You can give him his own spot where he's only allowed to dig. If he is digging on another spot, try directing him in his own digging spot and eventually he'll get used to it. If you want to further encourage him, try burying something there that he would like to dog out. You can try to put up a small sandbox where your dog can do the digging.

Excessive Barking

Excessive barking is a very common unpleasant behavior of dogs. But take note that this is a natural thing for them to do. To put a stop on this behavior, try to teach your dog the command to be quiet by using the words "quiet" or "shush" whenever they are barking excessively. If ever he stopped barking after you've said the words mentioned, give your dog a treat and praise him immediately to reinforce the command

Begging at the table

It is a bad habit for dogs to beg for food. So, it is better to prevent it firsthand. If you're going to eat, put your dog in his shelter or crate with a chew toy to keep him busy and let him out after you have finished eating. But if this behavior is already present, confine your dog while you are eating and let it bark and whine. Let him out only if he is quiet.

Chapter Seven: Showing Your Rottweilers

Rottweilers are very trainable especially if they undergo series of training since they were still young and they are charming as well. For this reason, this breed is eligible for competing in a dog show. If you are interested in showing off your dog's ability, why not sign up for a dog show competition? There are several kinds of dog shows you can choose from that would best suit your dog's capability. Through being a part of such competitions, you can bring out so much more potential for your pet than just being a house dog. All you have to do is to prepare your dog as well as yourself in order to bring home the victory.

In this chapter, you will learn more about the specific standard for the Rottweiler breed, and also some guiding principle on how to prepare your dog for a competition. This information will help you in making a decision whether letting your Rottweiler become a part of competitions is really something you want to do.

Competition Reminder:

Entering into dog shows is something you and your dog will enjoy. Plus, it can be a great training ground for your Rottweiler. In order to be a part of several dogs shows you must first be able to comply with the requirements. Usually, you must first request for a Schedule of the Show. You can personally get this at the event or from the Show Secretary. Then, fill out the Kennel Club with the necessary information about your dog. Submit it afterward with the appropriate fee.

Types of Dog Shows:

- **Companion Show**- this is the type of show wherein dogs can enter regardless if they are KC registered or not. These are usually held during summer in a place with a great ambiance where young puppies could socialize.
- **Limited Show**- this is exclusive for the members of the Show Society or to other exhibitors who are a resident of a specific area
- **All- Breed Championship Show**- this is a huge event and is usually held outdoors during summer time. During this event, there will be large marquees where the dogs are going to be benched. There will be different dog-related stalls all over the place. This usually lasts for three to four days.
- **Breed Championship Show**- the participants of this show are the same breed depending on what breed the organizers have set for the said competition.
- **Open Show**- this show includes dogs belonging to different breed classes. This can be a good opportunity for your dog if you are a novice handler.

Criteria for Judging

Head
- Dome-shaped skull
- Ears lying flat on the head against the cheeks
- Dark brown almond shaped eyes
- Muzzle is broad and strong
- With strong underjaw
- 2:3 ratio of the muzzle and skull
- Dark gums and lips

Dentition
- All 42 teeth are placed correctly
- Scissor-bite grip

Gait
- Powerful and economical gait
- Slow trot
- The head lowers with the chin parallel with the topline
- Behind the front is where the rear feet will track

Essentials
- Gender
- Bone and Substance
- Balance

- Topline
- Zygomatic Arch
- Stop
- Economical Gait
- Attitude

It's Showtime!

Becoming a part of dog shows can be a wonderful experience for you and for your dog but this can also be quite challenging. To make sure that your dog will do well, he needs to be in good physical and mental shape. Also, you must make sure that your dog's characteristics are aligned with the rules and regulations of the show you are about to join.

To ensure that your dog meets the breed standard, there are some factors you must take into account in order to be ready for the dog show. Below is the list of guidelines you must take into consideration before presenting your Rottweiler.

- Ensure that your dog is properly aligned with the pedigree required by the regulations of the show. There might be a need to present your dog's papers or license so make sure you bring them with you.

- Carefully fill out the registration form with all the information and necessary details and submit in on time.

- Prepare yourself to pay an entry fee as well or a competition fee if there's any

- Make sure that your dog is registered with the organization who held the show.

- Make yourself knowledgeable on the things that be provided by the show and what you need to bring for yourself

- Make sure that your dog belongs in the proper age bracket or category because some organizations have strict age requirements.

- Prepare yourself as you are about to spend the whole day at the show. Make sure you have everything you and your dog needs.

- Be mindful of all the information the show provides with your registration, some shows give a list of materials that you need to bring either through their website or it may be sent to your email.

Guidelines at the event

Of course, there are also things you must consider when you are in the location. Here it is:

- When you are in the event, do not slack but rather let your dog socialize with other pets.
- Be friendly with other pet owners. You may try to socialize with them. Remember, there's no harm in making new friends.
- Be confident. If you are a beginner do not be intimidated with other pet owners who are patrons in joining dog shows.
- Do not hesitate the stewards or volunteers around the event if ever you have questions.
- Do not be anxious about what's going to happen. Relax and just enjoy the moment.

Essential Stuff You Should Bring

Below are the lists of things you need to bring before the show:
- Your dog's pedigree, registration papers, and license.
- Veterinary records and proof of vaccinations.
- Enough food treats and water along with food/water bowls.

- Your dog's cage along with cage curtains and clips to hang them.
- Crate fan
- A blanket or comfy bed for the cage.
- Show lead and collar
- Any essential grooming equipment like nail clippers.
- Confirmation slip received at entry.
- Folding chair (if the event is outdoors)
- Plastic mats (if the event is outdoors)
- Food, water, and extra clothes for yourself.
- Garbage bag for clean-up.

Chapter Eight: Breeding Your Rottweilers

If you think you're ready in having new puppies playing around, maybe it's time for you to take a shot in breeding your pet Rottweiler. All you need to do is to know the correct process on how to breed them when the perfect time comes. Who knows? Maybe you could be one of the most highly regarded breeders of all time. In this chapter, you'll be aware and gain knowledge with information about sexual dimorphism for Rottweilers, breeding basics, their mating process, and the things you need to prepare for the newest addition to the family – puppies.

Sexual Dimorphism

Sexual dimorphism is the condition where differences between sexes are present and even go beyond their sexual organs. Rottweilers, just like any dogs and mammals, are generally sexually dimorphic meaning that their sex can be easily identified through their size, body structure, and other secondary sexual features. Of course, by looking at their sexual organs you can easily figure out if it's a male or female Rottweiler.

Breeding Basics

Just like most female creatures and even humans, dogs undergo estrous cycle or more commonly known as a heat cycle. Female dogs that are already sexually mature go through heat once or twice every year. They undergo such process when they reached the age of 9-12 months, but this may vary. There will be four stages consisting a female dog's heat cycle namely the proestrus stage, estrus stage, diestrus stage, and anestrus stage. The hormones estrogen, luteinizing hormone, and progesterone are the three hormones responsible for a female dog's estrous or heat cycle.

Dogs, unlike primates, do not undergo the stage of menopausal as they age but rather their heat cycles gradually stretch over time and so, the female dogs also called bitch will have heat cycles throughout their lifetime. They are also induced ovulators meaning that they will not undergo the process of ovulation unless they are bred with a male dog.

Signs that Your Female Dog is ready for Mating

There are several signs that will indicate that the bitch is undergoing heat cycle. If your female Rottweiler is acting upon such signs, it means that she is ready for mating and looking for a mate. Usually, male dogs will know if the bitch is ready for mating through the scent they give off while ovulating. You'll confirm whether your dog is ready for mating with the help of these signs:

- The genital area called vulva is swelling and there is a discharge of blood with a distinct smell.
- The rear area is more noticeable
- Urinating more frequently than the usual in small quantities
- Wanting to go outside more often than normal
- Letting the male dog or stud inspect her genital area

A female dog's entire heat cycle goes for about 21 days so expect these behaviors to last at such time, but this may vary. Each stage they undergo lasts between four and twelve days. This cycle will end as her body prepares for pregnancy if the bitch is bred.

Mating Process

It is advisable that you do not breed your female Rottweiler during the first stage of heat cycle to avoid putting your dog under stress. It is advisable that you breed them between the tenth and 14th day of the start of the proestrus stage. Mating your dog for a total of two or three times will be enough as long as your dog has already accepted its mate. Make sure that there's an allowance of one day for rest during the mating period. You may need a veterinarian to make sure that you will catch the peak fertile period of your dog for a bigger chance of conception. Signs of pregnancy may include an increase in weight, appetite, and nipple size.

All About Dog Pregnancy

The pregnancy of dogs is called gestation. The gestation period for Rottweilers last approximately for 63 days from the day of conception, but this may vary depending on the dog's litter size. Relatively, pregnancy in dogs is shorter compared to human pregnancy as it only lasts for about 9 weeks. Remember that each day matters and you really have to take care of your dog while waiting for the puppies to come out. Make sure that you keep your pregnant dog healthy. You may need the professional help of your veterinarian in order to properly monitor the pregnancy of your pet.

First Stage of Labor

Like humans, dogs undergo the process of labor while giving birth. There are three stages of labor they go through. On the first stage, their size of their cervix begins to dilate and contractions will begin. This stage can make your dog feel restless and uncomfortable. The contractions will be painful for your pet. This is the longest stage and it will last up to six to eighteen hours.

Second Stage of Labor

In the second stage of labor, the placental water sacks will break and you will notice a straw-colored fluid passing on the genital area of your dog. The puppies, in general, appear every half-hour or so. When the puppies have been born, the mother will lick them clean and will remove their umbilical cord through biting. With the help of the mother's licking, the puppies will be able to breathe properly and it improves their blood circulation.

Third Stage of Labor

The third and last stage of labor happens when the remaining placenta, blood, and fluid is expelled from the body of your female dog. During labor, there are some ways you can help your pet. Though it's not necessary to still it won't do any harm. But before anything else, make sure that you will seek your veterinarian's advice as to how you may help your dog properly during the period of their labor. Preparing a comfortable nesting would be a big help so that your dog will have her own private area on where she can give birth to her puppies.

In an average, Rottweilers can give birth to four to nine puppies, but this may vary. It can be less or even more. It is best for you to let your dog have an ultrasound in order for you to know how many puppies you should expect.

Dogs, in general, become mature after a year of their birth. Unlike other breeds, Rottweilers are not considered mature until they reach their second year of age. Be sure to cherish the moments while they are still puppies for when they mature, that's entirely a different phase to deal with.

Though you may see signs indicating that your dog is pregnant, it is recommended that you consult your veterinarian to make sure of it since there is a condition called Pseudo-pregnancy. It is the term used to denote false pregnancies of dogs. It happens when a non-pregnant female dog is showing the symptoms of pregnancy like abdominal distention, vomiting, increase in the size of its mammary glands, loss of appetite, restlessness, self-nursing, and other behavioral changes.

Quick Facts

Did you know that a dog can be impregnate by multiple fathers? A female dog can remain responsive to breeding for seven days or more when they are in the heat cycle. If by chance your dog mates with more than one male dog, the puppies in the litter might have different fathers

Raising Puppies

The usual scenario after your dog gives birth is the time where the mother spends time with her babies by nursing and feeding them through her mammary glands. Ensure that your dog has a comfortable bed where she can relax and take care of her puppies. Make sure that you will provide her with the right nutrition. Seek for your veterinarian's advice as to how you should take care of your dog that gave birth with regards its nutrition in order for her to recover and regain strength within a short period of time.

Have your puppies visit your veterinarian as soon as possible. They are more prone to catching different illness as they are still adjusting to their new environment and so you ensure that their health is properly monitored. Have to get the vaccinations they need when they reach the right age. You can also ask for your veterinarian's prescription regarding with the supplements your puppies may take in order for them to become healthy and strong. Ask the diet that will be suitable for your puppies in order to ensure that they will grow with the best health.

Make sure your new puppies will have a plenty time for rest in their comfortable safe area. They require a lot of sleep so make sure they get some. Spend time with your puppies and socialize with them. By this, you are decreasing the chance of aggression among the puppies' behavior. Set up a comfy bedding and make sure to place it near their mother in order to bond with her and for them to be able to be fed by her through her mammary glands.

Chapter Nine: Common Diseases and Health Requirements

In this chapter, you will be given information with some of the most common health problems affecting Rottweilers. If you are knowledgeable of the possible diseases and disorders that may cause trouble and even be fatal for your pet, it can be economic and potentially life-saving too! As the famous old saying goes, prevention is better than cure. You as a potential dog keeper should also come to know how to strengthen your dog's resistance to common illnesses by providing them the necessary vaccinations and also by letting them have a medical checkup with their veterinarians to ensure that they are free from any disease.

Health Problems of Rottweilers

In this section, you will be aware of the diseases that may affect and threaten your Rottweiler. Having knowledge of these as well as its remedies is essential for you and for your dog for the reason that you could prevent it from arising or even help with its treatment if by any chance it happens.

Rottweilers are prone to having orthopedic disorders, circulatory system diseases, eye problems, skin diseases and other common diseases. This can be avoided if you will take precautions and monitor your dog's health. A professional help from your vet is also ideal to ensure that your pet is living a healthy life. The conditions that are common for Rottweilers to have are the following:

Hip Dysplasia

This common joint problem is one form of arthritis. It is a type of deformity of the dog's hipbone. It is wherein the development of the socket joint of the dogs is growing abnormally. A healthy dog's thigh bone on the upper end fits perfectly into their hip bone that can facilitate a perfect and smooth movement and this is lacking on a dog who's suffering from this disorder. There's no age that this illness picks. Both old and young dogs can develop hip dysplasia.

This condition ranges from slight abnormality up to the worst which is the actual dislocation of the joint.

Panosteitis

Also known as "pano" or "long bone disease", is a type of illness that affects the dogs that are between five to twelve months of age. This disease only affects dogs coming from large or giant breeds. Dogs affected with this ailment suffer sporadic lameness of the limbs, one after the other, over several weeks or months. In this condition, there is an excessive bone production on the long bones found in the hind and front legs. This results in inflammation causing pain to your dog. This is a self-limiting disease and the symptoms usually withdraw when the dog reaches 20 months of age.

Elbow Dysplasia

This disease is actually a term used to denote a collection of elbow diseases that are congenital in dogs. This is characterized by the malformation of the joints causing abnormal development or damaging of the bone or cartilage thus, increasing the chance of having osteoarthritis. Rottweiler, being a medium-to-large size dog, is prone to catching this ailment. Dogs who are suffering from this disease have a front-limb lameness which varies on degrees. The lameness may develop as early as four months of age.

This can only be treated through a surgical procedure. Some of the specific elbow diseases are:

- *Osteochondritis Dissecans (OCD)*
  This is also known as canine OCD. It is a problem with the cartilage as it develops. This occurs usually in dogs ranging from six months to 2 years of age. Dogs suffering from canine OCD characterize lameness on the fore limbs.

- *Fragmented Coronoid Process (FCP)*
  This type is the most common elbow disease of dogs. It is a condition wherein the dog has a broken fragment of bones and cartilage on the ulna. The cause of this is still unknown.

- *Un-united Anconceal Process (UAP)*
  It is a condition wherein the anconeal process failed to unite with the ulna. This is a genetic disease characterized by an abnormal growth rate of the bones or joint found in the elbow.

Aortic Stenosis

This ailment is a congenital heart disease wherein the aorta narrows as it leaves the left ventricle. The reason for the narrowing is the presence of a scar-like tissue lying underneath the aortic valve causing the difficulty of the heart to pump blood to the body. This illness can be fatal. Dogs suffering from aortic stenosis have intolerance over exercise and in most serious cases; they faint during an exercise session.

Von Wilebrand's Disease (Vwd)

This disease is an inherited bleeding disorder affecting a few breeds like Rottweilers. The reason of the bleeding is the deficiency in the Von Wilebrand factor, a plasma protein that aids blood clot. Usually, the bleeding is only mild and it lessens as the dog grows old but there are cases that are severe that include bleeding beneath the skin, urine, stool and even prolonged nosebleeds. This can be a deadly disorder since even a minor wound would bleed out excessively. Unfortunately, there's no cure for this kind of illness. However, there are ways it can be managed like controlling the bleeding with the help of pressure wraps, bandages, skin glue, and sutures.

Progressive retinal atropy (PRA)

This is a hereditary disease characterized by the gradual deterioration of the retina. In the early stages, your dog might suffer poor night vision. As time goes by, the daytime vision of your pet will also fail. The lens of their eyes will become cloudy giving rise to cataract and their pupils will become dilated. Rottweilers with the age between two to five years might have night blindness and after a year or so it might progress to becoming totally blind. Unfortunately, Progressive retinal atropy does not have any treatment yet. In spite of this, blind dogs can make up for their illness with the help of their exceptional senses of hearing and smell.

Cataracts

This is also known as juvenile cataracts. This illness affects Rottweilers that are younger than six years old. This is when the crystalline lens of the eye became cloudy. Surgery is the treatment for this illness.

Eczema

If you can see swollen non-pigmented areas on the top layer of your dog's skin, he might be suffering from eczema. Your dog might frequently scratch the affected part as it calms them but this is something you must put into stop since it may cause the swelling of the skin as well as hair loss. Remember to always check the skin of your dog to trace this disease at its earliest stage.

Seborrhea

The reason of the development of this skin disease is the hyperactivity of your dog's sebaceous gland causing an excessive fat accumulation in the skin. This is characterized by the accumulation of loose fats and hilly. If you're not able to treat this at the early stage, this might progress and lead to eczema

Dermatitis

This is a condition wherein the layers of the skin are all under the state of inflammation without the appearance of rashes. The common symptoms of this ailment are swelling or the skin and depression. Chronic dermatitis includes the sealing of thickened skin. This can actually be cured with the help of massages, paraffin baths, and ultrasound therapy. While purulent dermatitis can be healed with through the utilization of bandages and compresses.

Minor Health Problem for Rottweilers:

Bloat

Known as gastric dilatation and volvulus in the fields of medicine, this is a serious medical condition that can cause death within a few hours if not treated properly and immediately. This refers to the condition wherein the stomach is filled with air causing to put pressure on the diaphragm and other organs making it hard for your dog to breathe properly. This is fatal as it has the ability to block the blood from flowing into the organs and when this happens the stomach tissues will deteriorate and the stomach will rupture. It is essential to seek for your veterinarian's help as soon as possible if ever your dog shows the symptoms of bloat.

Recommended Vaccinations

Even though dogs are healthy, it is highly recommended that you provide them the vaccinations they need to be fully protected against certain diseases. Vaccines are primarily divided into two classes namely the core vaccines and the noncore vaccines.

Core vaccines are the ones that should be given to all the dogs. On the other hand, noncore vaccines are the ones recommended for a specific dog depending on its breed, health status, and exposure time of the dog with others who are suffering from a certain illness, and age.

The AVMA Council on Biologic and Therapeutic Agents has suggested the following vaccines:

Core Vaccines
- Canine adenovirus-2
- Distemper
- Canine parvovirus-2

- Rabies

Noncore Vaccines
- Coronavirus
- Leptospirosis
- Borrelia burgdorferi
- Bordetetella bronchiseptica

Vaccination Schedule for Dogs and Puppies

When your puppy has turned five-week old, the risk of your dog having a parvovirus is very high. For this reason, this is the recommended time for a vaccination against parvovirus but this may vary. You may ask for your veterinarian's advice if your puppy is ready for this kind of vaccine.

A puppy aged six to 9 weeks is suggested to have a combination vaccine, also known as a 5-way vaccine, which usually includes hepatitis, adenovirus cough, distemper, parvovirus, and parainfluenza, as well as a vaccine for coronavirus on which by this age is a serious concern.

By the time your dog reaches 12 weeks of age, you should provide him with a vaccine for rabies. This may be given by your local veterinarian. Be mindful that the age with the vaccination for rabies varies depending on the local law present.

When they reach the age of twelve to fifteen weeks, they may be given a combination vaccine along with vaccine for leptospirosis, lyme, and coronavirus.
For adults, they may be given boosters to lower the risk of diseases. They can be administered with a combination vaccine together with a vaccine for leptospirosis, coronavirus, rabies, and lyme.

The vaccinations needed by dogs may vary and so it is necessary to discuss with your local veterinarian regarding the appropriate vaccination schedule for your dog. Keep in mind that recommendations vary depending on the breed, age, and health status of the cat, the potential of the cat to be exposed to the disease, whether the dog is used for breeding, the type of vaccine, and the geographical area where the dog lives.

Chapter Ten: Care Sheet and Summary

As an owner, it is your responsibility to give what's best for your pet. Therefore, you must also do some research for you to know more about the breed you chose, some other techniques you might use in order to maintain a happy and healthy life for them, etc. In this chapter, we will give you the quick synopsis of the major points you need to keep in mind that was discussed in this book. This can be helpful if you want to check out on a specific topic without the need to further read the whole book again. Thank you for reading! We hope that you learned and will learn more.

Biological Information

Taxonomy: Kingdom Animalia, Phylum Chordata, Class Mammalia, Order Carnivora, Family Canidae, Genus Canis, and Species Lupus Familiaris
Country of Origin: Germany

Breed Size: medium – to-large breed
Body Type and Appearance: Has an athletic muscular body and a large and broad head
Weight: average of 95-130 lbs (males), average of 85-115 lbs (females)
Coat Length: medium-length coat
Coat Texture: smooth and glossy

Color: black coat with tan markings

Other name: Rottie, Rottweiler Metzgerhund

Rottweilers as Pets

Temperament: ranging from serious, reserved, and self-assured to affectionate and silly
Other pets: can get along with other pets but some are predatory towards cats
Major Pro: very clever, easy to train, responsive

Major Con: can be potentially aggressive when not socialized properly

Legal Requirements and Dog Licensing:

United States: There are no federal requirements for licensing either cats or even dogs. It is regulated only at the state level.

United Kingdom: Licensing for dogs is mandatory and there will be a need to get a special permit if you plan to travel with your dog into or out of the country.

Other countries: You will need to bring proper documents such as your state permit for your dog, current health condition, and rabies or vaccinations certificate. Other requirements may be needed depending on the policy of the place you are about to visit with your pet.

Purchasing and Selecting a Healthy Breed

Where to Purchase: Private Breeders, Online Stores, Dog Conventions

Characteristics of a Reputable Breeder: You can determine that you are associating yourself with a reputable breeder if he also asks you questions about yourself. A responsible breeder wants to make sure that his dogs go to good and safe homes.

Characteristics of a Healthy Breed: Examine dog's or puppy's physique thoroughly and look for any signs of illness and potential injuries. The puppy should be playful, active, socializing with each other in a healthy way and not shying away.

Habitat Requirements for Rottweilers :The bigger the comfy bed you can provide, the better for your pet! Provide play pen, perches, toys and other essential accessories. Make sure to make their environment comfortable

Housing Temperature: They should not be exposed where the temperature is more than 35 C. The temperature that fits with its tolerance is ranging from 0 C to 25 C.

Nutrition and Food

Rottweiler must be given primarily protein – rich foods along with some healthy fats as part of their nutritional diet.

Recommended Brands of Rottweiler Foods: Blue Buffalo Wilderness Salmon Recipe. I and Love You Nude Food Red Meat, Innova Nature's Table Grain Free Ranch-Raised Beef & Red Lentils, Black Wood Chicken Meal & Rice Recipe, Eukanuba Rottweiler Dog Food

How to Feed Your Rottweiler: Read and follow the Feeding Instructions and Recommended Daily Feeding Amounts found on the packaging of your pet food. You may also seek the advice of your veterinarian regarding the right amount of food for your dog.

Feeding Amount/Frequency: Their energy levels, previous conditions, size, age, weight etc. should be taken into account as to the amount needed to feed your dog. It's highly recommended that you consult your vet in order to ensure that your pet gets all the nutrition it needs for the reason that they can identify what your pet needs in terms of its daily diet, the proper food ratio, and the frequency.

Grooming and Training Your Rottweilers

How to Brush Your Dog's Teeth: It is recommended that you should brush your dog's teeth every day

How to Trim Your Dog's Nails: Once a week or twice a month will be enough.

Cleaning Your Dog's Ears: It is advisable that you clean your dog's ears occasionally in order for you to remove normal wax buildup. You may use a dog ear cleaning solution and squeeze a few drops into the ear canal.

Showing Your Rottweilers:

Types of Shows
- Companion Show
- Limited Show
- All-Breed Championship Show
- Breed Championship Show
- Open Show

Criteria for Judging

- Head
- Dentition
- Gait
- Essentials

Breeding Your Rottweilers

Gestation Period: 63 days from the time of conception

Litter Size: Female Rottweilers usually give birth to four to nine puppies, but this may vary

Maturity: Puppies mature when they reach 2 years of age

Common Diseases of Rottweilers

- **Bone – Related Disorders:** Hip Dysplasia, Panosteitis, Elbow Dysplasia (Osteochondritis Dissecans, Fragmented Coronoid Process, Un-united Anconceal Process).
- **Circulatory System Diseases:** Von Wilebrand's Disease (Vwd), Aortic Stenosis
- **Eye Disorders:** Progressive Retinal Atropy (PRA), Cataracts
- **Skin Diseases:** Eczema, Seborrhea, Dermatitis
- **Minor Health Problems:** Bloat

Recommended Vaccinations for Rottweilers Pups:

Core Vaccines
- Canine adenovirus-2
- Distemper
- Canine parvovirus-2
- Rabies

Noncore Vaccines
- Coronavirus
- Leptospirosis
- Borrelia burgdorferi
- Bordetetella bronchiseptica

Glossary of Dog Terms

Achondroplasia: Abnormal development of cartilage found at the ends of the long bones; resulting to a congenital dwarfism.

Acquired Immunity: Immunity achieved through the injection of antiserum or development of antibodies.

Agility Trials: Competition organized at which dogs undergo a series of obstacles and jumps.

All-Breed Show: A type of conformation show where all AKC-recognized breeds are allowed to be exhibited.

Almond Eyes: Shape of the eyes that are elongated rather than rounded

American Kennel Club: It is an organization founded and established in line with the laws of the State of New York for purebred dogs events

Barrel Hocks: A.k.a spread hocks, a type of hocks that turn out

Barring: Markings that are stripes

Beady: Used to describe small, round, and glittering eyes.

Beard: The long hair growing and can be seen on the underjaw.

Collar: A material used to restrain a dog. Usually made from nylon, leather or chain. It is also where the leash is attached.

Colitis: A kind of inflammation in the colon.

Dermatitis: A kind of Inflammation in the skin.

Distemper: A viral disease of dogs that is very infectious often characterized by a catarrhal discharge from the eyes and nose, loss of appetite, vomiting, fever, and partial paralysis.

Dog Fancy: Used to denote a group of people who are actively interested in the promotion of purebred dogs.

Dog Show: Also called as conformation show, It is where dogs are judged on how closely they met their own breed standards

Enteritis: A kind of inflammation in the intestinal tract

Entropion: A genetic condition that is complexly resulting in the turning in of the eyelid; causes corneal ulceration.

Even Bite: Also known as the level bite, it means the meeting of upper and lower incisors exactly.

Fallow: Pale cream to light fawn color; pale yellow; yellow-red. Color definitions may vary by breed. Always check the breed standard for the definitive color description.

Feathering: It is the long fringe of hair found on the legs, ears, body, or tail.

Flying Ears: It is characterized by semi-prick ears and drop ears that can stand or fly

Gait: It is the walk in general or the pattern of footsteps at various rates of speed

Groom: Keeping the neatness of your dog by means of brushing, combing, or trimming

Groups: Includes the groups that the AKC has made; working, toy, sporting, hound, non-sporting, herding, and terrier

Hip Dysplasia: It is a condition wherein the hip joint is abnormally formed

Hormone: It is usually a peptide or steroid that may be responsible growth or metabolism.

Humane Societies: Groups advocating to fight and stop animal and human abuse

Hypothermia: A condition wherein the body is exposed to a very cold environment causing an abnormally low body temperature

Inbreeding: It is the mating of two dogs who are closely related and of the same breed.

Inflammation: It refers to the redness, pain, and swelling of the skin tissues caused by injury, irritation, or infection.

Injection: It refers to a dose of liquid medicine that is being injected into the body.

Iris: It is a colored membrane neighboring the pupil of the eye.

Jacobson's Organ: It is a sense organ found in the roof of the dog's mouth. The function of this organ is between smell and taste.

Jowls: It is the flesh of the jaws and lips

Kennel: An enclosed building where dogs are being kept.

Kennel Cough: Also known as Tracheobronchitis of dogs

Kink Tail: It is characterized by a deformity in the caudal vertebrae

Knuckling Over: It is a condition wherein the wrist joint is faulty structured allowing it to flex forward due to the standing dog's weight

Leather: It denotes the ear's flap or the outer ear buoyed by cartilage and surrounding tissue.

Leptospirosis: A kind of disease that is infectious to domestic animals.

Luxating Patella: Th condition wherein the kneecap slips when the joint is moved. This problem is transmitted genetically and can potentially lead to lameness

Luxation: Anatomical structure's dislocation

Maternal Immunity: A kind immunity that is temporary and can be passed from a mother to her offspring while inside the uterus

Microchip: A device as small as a grain of rice encoded with a unique number. This is implanted underneath the skin of your dog.

Molars: It is the posterior teeth of the dental arcade, with two on each side of the upper jaw and three on each side in the lower jaw in an adult with correct dentition.

Natural Breed: This refers when a breed of dog occurred naturally even without the need for selective breeding.

Neuter: The process of castrating or spaying.

Nick: A kind breeding that can produce desirable puppies.

Nictitating Membrane: It is the inner eyelids of some mammals, birds, and reptiles that are transparent. Also known as the third eyelid.

Obedience Trial: This is an event in line with the rules of AKC at which an obedience degree can be merited

Obesity: It is a condition characterized by an excessive accumulation of fat leading to the state of being overweight or obese.

Omnivore: A person or animal that eats both vegetable and animal substances

Ovulate: The process of producing ova or the discharging of eggs from the ovary

Parvovirus: A disease of canines that is highly contagious and fatal.

Pedigree: It is a record of a dog's genealogy of three generations or more which is usually written.

Phenotype: It is the observable biochemical or physical characteristics of an organism determined with the help of environmental influences and genetic makeup.

Quarantine: Enforced isolation or restriction of free movement imposed to prevent the spread of contagious disease.

Quick: It is the vein that runs through a dog's nails or claw

Registries: These are the organizations responsible for keeping the official records on specific subjects with respect to dogs.

Reward: It is something positive like treats or praise usually utilized as a motivating factor to stimulate desired behavior

Saddle: These are the markings in the shape of a saddle that can be found on the back.

Scent: It is the odor left by any animal in trail

Shock: A massive physiological reaction that is temporarily caused by severe emotional or physical trauma.

Show Quality: A dog pedigreed to meet the official breed standard, therefore, becoming fit to compete in dog shows.

Topical: A kind of drug applied on a localized surface of the body

Topline: The outline of the dog from behind the withers up to the tail

Trail: Hunting through smelling the scent of the ground

Undercoat: A soft and dense short coat covered by a longer top coat.

Underline: A combination of contours in connection with the brisket and the abdominal floor.

Utility Dog (UD): A dog rewarded by the AKC as a Utility Dog in line with his winnings towards certain minimum scores.

Vaccine: It is a preparation towards killed or weakened pathogen, usually a bacterium or virus

Walk: It is the gaiting pattern wherein three legs are supporting the body at all times on which feet are lifting on the ground in a regular sequence

Wind: Catching the scent of game.

Winging: A fault in the gaiting on which one or both front feet twist outward while the limbs are swinging forward.

Xiphoid Process: The sternum's cartilage process

Zoonosis: Used to denote certain disease of animals that can be easily transmitted to humans like rabies or psittacosis

Zygomatic Arch: It is a ridge that is bony extending posteriorly from under the eye orbit.

Index

C

D

H

I

K

L

Q

R

S

T

U

V

W

Photo Credits

References

" A Guide to Choosing Your Rottweiler Puppy"
Pethelpful.com
< https://pethelpful.com/dogs/A-Guide-to-Choosing-your-Rottweiler-Puppy>

"All You Need To Know About Dog Mating"
Pethelpful.com
< https://pethelpful.com/dogs/Dog-Mating>

"Are Rottweilers Good With Other Cats & Dogs"
Rottweilerhope.org
< http://www.rottweilerhope.org/are-rottweilers-good-with-other-cats-dogs.html>

"Best Dog Food For Rottweilers" Herepup.com
< https://herepup.com/best-dog-food-for-rottweilers/>

"Cataracts in Dogs" Petmd.com
< http://www.petmd.com/dog/conditions/eye/c_dg_cataract>
"Criteria for Best in Show Dog Judging" Cuteness.com
< https://www.cuteness.com/blog/content/criteria-for-best-in-show-dog-judging>

"Diet and Nutrition of Your Rottweiler"
Rottweilersonline.com

< http://www.rottweilersonline.com/health-and-diet/diet-and-nutrition-your-rottweiler>

"Dog Food" Mydogspace.com
< http://www.mydogspace.com/dog-food-3-types-of-standard-commercial-dog-food-sold-in-stores/>

"Dog Licensing and Microchipping" Nidirect.gov.uk
< https://www.nidirect.gov.uk/articles/dog-licensing-and-microchipping>

"Dog- Proofing Your Home" Thebark.com
<http://thebark.com/content/dog-proofing-your-home-room-room-guide?page=2>

"Foods That Are Bad For Dogs" Dogtime.com
< http://dogtime.com/dog-health/general/5504-bad-foods-for-dogs-list>
"Fruits & Vegetables That Are Toxic to Dogs"
Iheartdogs.com
< https://iheartdogs.com/10-fruits-vegetables-that-are-toxic-to-dogs/3/>

"How to Feed a Dog" Wikihow.pet
< http://www.wikihow.pet/Feed-a-Dog>

"How to Help Your Dog Whelp or Deliver Puppies" Wikihow.com <http://www.wikihow.com/Help-Your-Dog-Whelp-or-Deliver-Puppies>

"How To Pick A Rottweiler Puppy" Pets.thenest.com < http://pets.thenest.com/pick-rottweiler-puppy-4243.html>

"How to Train a Dog" Wikihow.com < http://www.wikihow.com/Train-a-Dog>

"Importance of A Healthy Diet" Rottweilerhq.com < https://www.rottweilerhq.com/importance-of-healthy-diet/>

"Pet Shop Puppies" Yourpurebredpuppy.com <http://www.yourpurebredpuppy.com/buying/articles/petshops-and-pet-stores.html>

"People Foods That Can Be Dangerous to Dogs" Dogfoodadvisor.com < https://www.dogfoodadvisor.com/people-foods-dangerous-dogs/>

"Poisonous Dog Food" Rottweilerhq.com < https://www.rottweilerhq.com/poisonous-dog-food/>

"Rottweiler" Dogtime.com
< http://dogtime.com/dog-breeds/rottweiler#/slide/1>

"Rottweiler Appearance" Rottweiler.wordpress.com
< https://rottweiler.wordpress.com/2006/09/12/rottweiler-appearance/>

"Rottweilers Appearance & Grooming" Petwave.com
<http://www.petwave.com/Dogs/Breeds/Rottweiler/Appearance.aspx>

"Rottweiler Dog Breed Information" Allourpaws.com
< http://allourpaws.com/pet-profiles/rottweiler/>

"Rottweiler Health Problems" Dogzhealth.com
< http://www.dogzhealth.com/rottweiler-health-problems.html>

"Rottweiler Pros and Cons of Owning This Surprising Pet" Ezinearticles.com
< http://ezinearticles.com/?Rottweiler-Pros-and-Cons-of-Owning-This-Surprising-Pet&id=6559354>

"Rottweiler Temperament" Yourpurebredpuppy.com
http://www.yourpurebredpuppy.com/reviews/rottweilers.html

"Suitable Temperature for Rottweilers" Anniemany.com
< http://www.anniemany.com/2013/04/suitable-temperature-for-rottweilers.html>

"Ten Tips for Showing Your Dog" Dogs.lovetoknow.com
< http://dogs.lovetoknow.com/dog-information/ten-tips-showing-your-dog>

"Tips for Dog Proofing Your Home" Rover.com
< https://www.rover.com/dog-proofing-your-home/>

"The Cost of Dog Ownership" Thespruce.com
< https://www.thespruce.com/the-cost-of-dog-ownership-1117321>

"The Rottweiler Club" Therottweilerclub.co.uk
< http://www.therottweilerclub.co.uk/the-breed/history-of-the-breed/>
"Von Warterr Rottweilers" Vonwarterr.net
< https://www.vonwarterr.net/current-rottweiler-litters>

"Your Guide to Rottweiler Grooming" A-love-of-rottweilers.com
< http://www.a-love-of-rottweilers.com/rottweiler-grooming.html>

Feeding Baby
Cynthia Cherry
978-1941070000

Axolotl
Lolly Brown
978-0989658430

Dysautonomia, POTS
Syndrome
Frederick Earlstein
978-0989658485

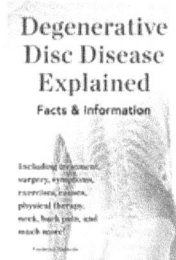

Degenerative Disc
Disease Explained
Frederick Earlstein
978-0989658485

Sinusitis, Hay Fever,
Allergic Rhinitis Explained
Frederick Earlstein
978-1941070024

Wicca
Riley Star
978-1941070130

Zombie Apocalypse
Rex Cutty
978-1941070154

Capybara
Lolly Brown
978-1941070062

Eels As Pets
Lolly Brown
978-1941070167

Scabies and Lice Explained
Frederick Earlstein
978-1941070017

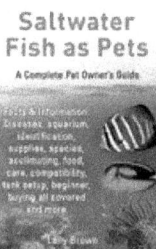

Saltwater Fish As Pets
Lolly Brown
978-0989658461

Torticollis Explained
Frederick Earlstein
978-1941070055

Kennel Cough
Lolly Brown
978-0989658409

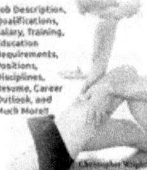

Physiotherapist, Physical
Therapist
Christopher Wright
978-0989658492

Rats, Mice, and Dormice
As Pets
Lolly Brown
978-1941070079

Wallaby and Wallaroo Care
Lolly Brown
978-1941070031

Bodybuilding Supplements
Explained
Jon Shelton
978-1941070239

Demonology
Riley Star
978-19401070314

Pigeon Racing
Lolly Brown
978-1941070307

Dwarf Hamster
Lolly Brown
978-1941070390

Cryptozoology
Rex Cutty
978-1941070406

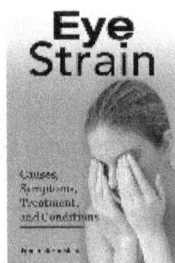

Eye Strain
Frederick Earlstein
978-1941070369

Inez The Miniature Elephant
Asher Ray
978-1941070353

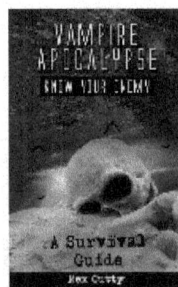

Vampire Apocalypse
Rex Cutty
978-1941070321